Producing Meat

Rachel Lynette

www.raintreepublishers.co.uk
Visit our website to find out more information about Raintree books.

To order:
☎ Phone 0845 6044371
🖹 Fax +44 (0) 1865 312263
🖨 Email myorders@raintreepublishers.co.uk

Customers from outside the UK please telephone +44 1865 312262

Raintree is an imprint of Capstone Global Library Limited, a company incorporated in England and Wales having its registered office at 7 Pilgrim Street, London, EC4V 6LB – Registered company number: 6695582

Edited by Abby Colich, Megan Cotugno, and Nancy Dickmann
Designed by Victoria Allen
Picture research by Elizabeth Alexander
Illustrations by Oxford Designers & Illustrators
Originated by Capstone Global Library Ltd
Printed and bound in China by China Translation and Printing Services Ltd

ISBN 978 1 406 24053 5
16 15 14 13 12
10 9 8 7 6 5 4 3 2 1

British Library Cataloguing in Publication Data
Lynette, Rachel.
  Producing meat. -- (The technology of farming)
  1. Meat animals--Juvenile literature. 2. Animal culture--Juvenile literature. 3. Meat industry and trade--Juvenile literature. 4. Agricultural innovations--Juvenile literature.
  I. Title II. Series
  636.2'13-dc23
A full catalogue record for this book is available from the British Library.

Acknowledgements
We would like to thank the following for permission to reproduce photographs: Alamy: pp. 11 (© AGStockUSA), 17 (© PhotoEdit), 21 (© SuperStock), 31 (© Felix Zaska); Corbis: pp. 8 (© Radius Images), 13 (© moodboard), 29 (© Hans Deryk/Reuters), 30 (© Philippe Henry/First Light), 41 (© Karen Kasmauski); Getty Images: pp. 15 (Danita Delimont/Gallo Images), 33 (Wirelmage/Bennett Raglin), 34 (Samuel Aranda/AFP), 35 (Carola Bravo/Bloomberg), 37 (Juan Mabromata/AFP), 39 (Keren Su/Stone), 43 (Mark Mawson/Robert Harding); image courtesy of Dr Athol Klieve: p. 38; Photolibrary: p. 7 (The British Library); Shutterstock: pp. 4 (© Martin Nemec), 12 (© LianeM), 14 (© Frontpage), 18 (© Weldon Schloneger), 22 (© Dario Sabljak), 25 (© Phant), 26 (© Flock of sheep).

Cover photo of chicken in a pen reproduced with permission from Getty Images (Javier Pierini/Photographer's Choice).

Every effort has been made to contact copyright holders of any material reproduced in this book. Any omissions will be rectified in subsequent printings if notice is given to the publisher.

Contents

Some words appear in the text in bold, **like this**. You can find out what they mean by looking in the glossary.

Where does meat come from?

When was the last time you ate meat? Did you have bacon or sausage for breakfast, or sliced chicken in your sandwich? Maybe you had a beefburger for dinner or a slice of meat. Before it was on your plate, that meat was an animal that was reared on a farm.

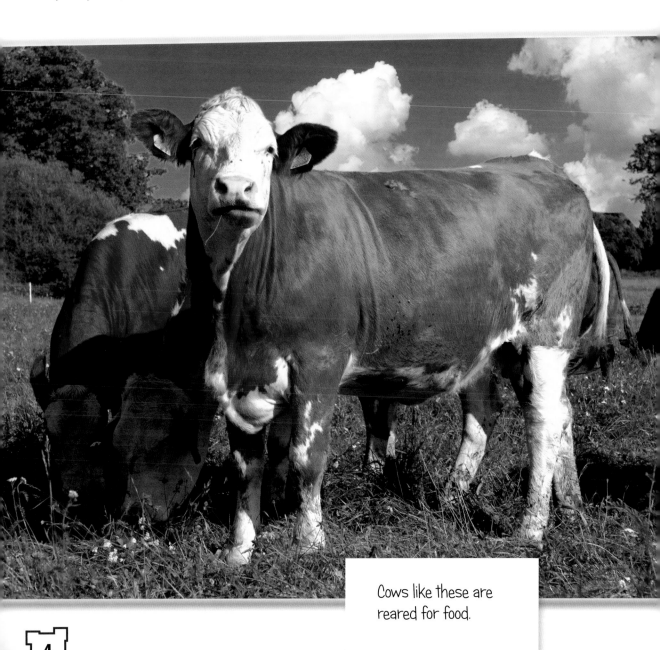

Cows like these are reared for food.

Lots of livestock

The **livestock** industry is one of the largest industries on our planet. Worldwide, it feeds billions of people and employs 1.3 billion people. That means that about one in every five people on Earth work in some aspect of the livestock industry.

In many developed countries such as the United States, the majority of livestock are reared on large factory farms called **concentrated animal feeding operations (CAFOs)**. A CAFO houses large numbers of the same kind of animal in a relatively small space, usually indoors. Feeding, temperature, and waste disposal must be carefully controlled. The largest CAFOs house **poultry** and contain more than 125,000 chickens at one time!

In **developing countries**, many people still keep small herds of animals on small farms or even in their back gardens. In this way, families can produce meat to feed themselves as well as to sell to neighbours or at the local market. However, as these countries develop, gaining better technologies and reliable long-distance transportation, more animals are being reared on CAFOs. In most cases, it costs less money to keep an animal in a CAFO than on a farm, so once the animal is slaughtered, its meat can be sold at a lower price.

What is the history of meat farming?

People began to **domesticate** animals more than 12,000 years ago in Europe, the Middle East, and Asia. They began by capturing wild animals. Then they bred them to encourage specific **traits** such as small horns, larger size, and mild **temperament**. Unlike hunting, domesticated animals provided these first farmers with a consistent food source. Many animals that we eat today, such as chickens, sheep, and pigs, were domesticated thousands of years ago.

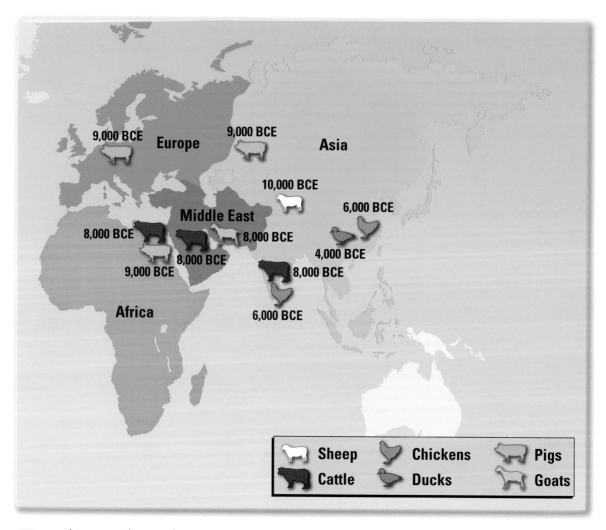

9,000 BCE Europe   9,000 BCE   Asia

10,000 BCE

6,000 BCE

Middle East

8,000 BCE   8,000 BCE

4,000 BCE

8,000 BCE

9,000 BCE   8,000 BCE

Africa   6,000 BCE

	Sheep		Chickens		Pigs
	Cattle		Ducks		Goats

This map shows where some animals first became domesticated.

This illustration shows sheep and their farmers in the 1300s.

Feudal farming

By the AD 6th century, the **feudal system** dominated Europe. Under the feudal system, rich lords owned most of the land. The majority of the population were poor peasants or serfs who were allowed to live on the land in exchange for their labour. Although they were given small plots to farm for their own use, most of their days were spent working in the lord's fields.

A variety of animals were reared for meat during this time, including ducks, pigeons, geese, chickens, partridges, pigs, cows, and sheep. Serfs grazed their animals on common pastures. Everyone in the family helped care for the animals; however, in many cases they rarely got to eat the animals they reared. Instead, the meat was taken by the lord to be used at large feasts in his manor. The feudal system deteriorated when the **bubonic plague** killed half the population of Europe in the 14th and 15th centuries and those left alive started to demand payment for their work.

Barbed wire

Barbed wire was invented by Joseph Glidden in 1874. It revolutionized fencing for livestock, but some people felt it was cruel to the animals.

Barbed wire made it much easier for farmers to fence in their animals.

Farming in the colonies

Before Europeans settled in the Americas, American Indians had been getting most of their meat from hunting bison and other wild animals. However, they had also been rearing turkeys for thousands of years. In South America, guinea pigs and alpacas were also kept for meat.

European settlers went to North and South America as well as Australia and New Zealand. They took their **livestock** and farming methods with them. Most of the meat eaten in those countries today comes from that original livestock of many generations ago. Many European colonists started family farms and kept small flocks of chickens and other farm animals. By the 1800s, the settlers had killed most of the buffalo as well as many of the American Indians on the plains of North America. The land was used as open grazing for cattle, which were reared on large ranches. There were also many large ranches in Argentina and Brazil.

In Australia and New Zealand, settlers brought cattle, sheep, and other livestock. They took land from the **Aboriginal people** who, rather than farming, had lived by hunting and gathering for thousands of years.

Mass production

In the early 1900s, advances in transportation and refrigeration made it possible to distribute meat all over the world. After World War II (1939–1945), with the introduction of fast food, there was a bigger demand for meat. In some countries, small family farms gave way to larger farm operations.

How is beef farmed?

The United States produces more beef than any other country. About 34 million cattle are slaughtered in the United States each year. Brazil, China, India, Argentina, and Australia are also big beef producers.

The science of growing cattle

To produce inexpensive meat, farmers on large-scale factory farms must rear cattle that grow very quickly. Several technologies are used to achieve this goal. On most farms, cattle spend the first part of their lives grazing on grass. However, during their last few months of life they are housed on large **feedlots** and fed a scientifically designed mix of grains so they will gain weight quickly. Cattle on feedlots gain up to 1.8 kilograms (4 pounds) per day.

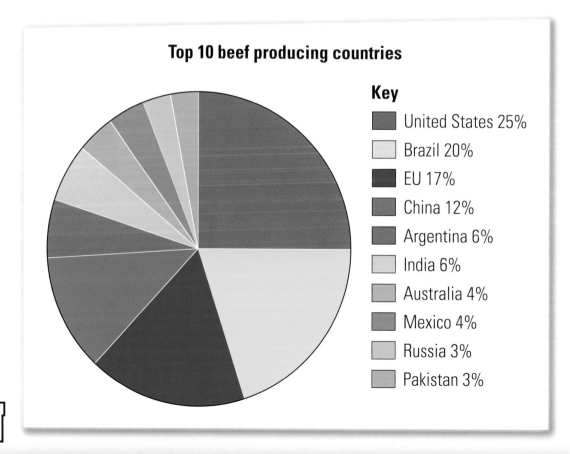

Top 10 beef producing countries

Key

- United States 25%
- Brazil 20%
- EU 17%
- China 12%
- Argentina 6%
- India 6%
- Australia 4%
- Mexico 4%
- Russia 3%
- Pakistan 3%

These cattle are eating grain that has been engineered to make them grow quickly.

This grain-rich diet combined with the crowded feedlot conditions leave the cattle vulnerable to diseases. Cattle in the US are given **antibiotics** to fight these diseases. The antibiotics also promote faster growth.

In the United States, cattle are also given **growth hormones**, which not only make them grow faster but also improve the meat so that it is less fatty. However, there are concerns that meat produced using growth hormones can cause serious health problems. Growth hormones are banned in the UK and Europe, so US beef cannot be sold there.

Electric cattle prod

Cattle farmers routinely use high-voltage electric prods to get animals to move. Although the shock is not strong enough to kill a human or cow, it is still very painful, and many people are against the use of electric cattle prods.

Sustainable beef

Sustainable farms use traditional farming methods in order to minimize harmful effects on the environment, people, and animals. Sustainable beef farms rear cattle without hormones, antibiotics, or engineered grains. Instead, small herds graze on open pastures, and their manure is used as **fertilizer**. In most cases, sustainable beef costs significantly more than beef from **CAFOs**; however, many consumers are willing to pay extra for meat that was reared **humanely** without antibiotics or growth hormones.

Albert Howard developed a composting method that is still in use today.

Albert Howard 1873–1947

Born in Shropshire in 1873, Albert Howard was a **botanist** and a pioneer in organic farming. When Howard was sent to India to teach the people there how to use Western farming technologies, he soon realized that he could learn more about healthy farming practices from them. He developed a method of **composting** as well as other organic farming techniques. He is the author of many important books on agriculture.

Organic challenges

Sustainable beef is not necessarily **organic** beef. A farm must be certified organic in order for the beef to be labelled organic. In order to be certified, organic beef farmers must follow strict regulations, which include making sure all cattle feed is certified organic. That means that no chemical fertilizers or **pesticides** can be used on the grazing pastures. In addition, organically reared cattle must have constant access to outdoor grazing land. Many farmers cannot meet all of the requirements. While the meat from their farms may be natural and sustainable, it cannot be labelled organic.

These cows are being reared sustainably.

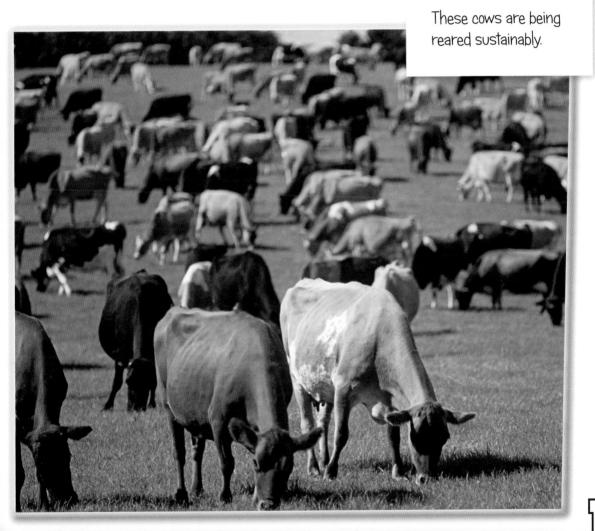

Grass fed in Brazil

Brazil is the world's largest beef exporter. There are about 200 million beef cattle in Brazil. These animals spend their days grazing in pasturelands. Unlike cattle in the United States, they are not kept on feedlots and fed grain and antibiotics. This is one reason why the demand for Brazilian beef is high.

Unfortunately, Brazil's dominance in the world meat market has taken a high toll on the Amazon rainforest. Large parts of the rainforest have been destroyed to make more room for grazing pastures. Brazil plans to double its beef production by 2018, which means that even more rainforest will be destroyed.

These cattle are grazing on land that was once rainforest.

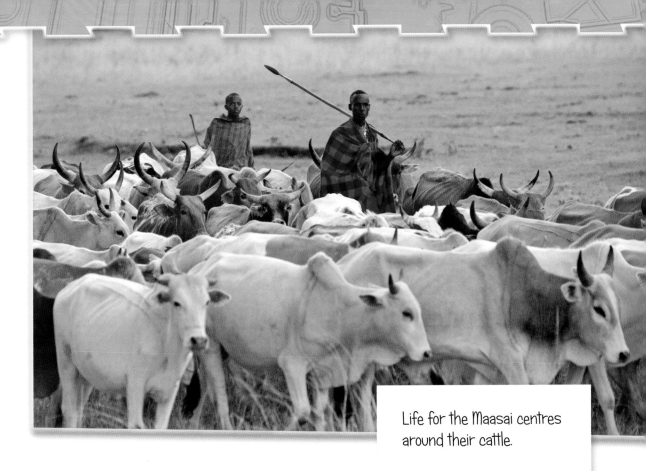

Life for the Maasai centres around their cattle.

Cattle as a way of life for the Maasai

The Maasai are an **indigenous** people living in Kenya and Tanzania. In many ways, the life of the Maasai centres around their cattle. Cows are the Maasai's primary food source. They not only drink cows' milk and eat cows' meat, they also occasionally drink cows' blood. A mixture of cows' blood and milk is used for rituals, and given to people who are ill. The number of cattle a man owns defines both his wealth and his status. The Maasai are a **nomadic** people, travelling with their herds to find water and grazing land.

The Maasai believe that cattle were created by their god specifically for their use. The Maasai have lost much of their land to the Kenyan government which has used the land to create wildlife preserves. They have also suffered huge losses from **droughts**, which have become more common in recent years.

How is poultry farmed?

Although chicken is the most popular kind of **poultry**, people also eat turkey, duck, ostrich, partridge, and a variety of other birds. Chickens bred for meat are called **broilers**. In the past, most of the world's chickens were kept in people's backyards for family consumption, and perhaps to sell at the local market. Today nearly three-fourths of all broilers worldwide are reared in huge chicken houses on **CAFOs**. The United States produces more poultry than any other country. China and Brazil also produce large amounts of poultry.

Cecile Steele

Cecile Steele from Delaware, USA, is often called the mother of the modern poultry industry. She was the first to farm large numbers of broilers. When the poultry company accidently sent 500 chicks instead of 50 to her farm in 1923, rather than sending them back she took on the challenge of rearing them all. She found her new business so profitable that within five years she and her husband were rearing 27,000 chickens at a time.

Plenty of poultry

In the United States, broilers are hatched in large **incubators**. Thousands of chickens live in crowded, windowless chicken houses. During their six to eight weeks of life, they eat feed that has been engineered for maximum growth. The feed also includes **antibiotics** to fight diseases that are caused by the **unsanitary** conditions. Many people feel it is **unethical** to rear chickens under these conditions. European countries have different, and often higher, standards for rearing poultry.

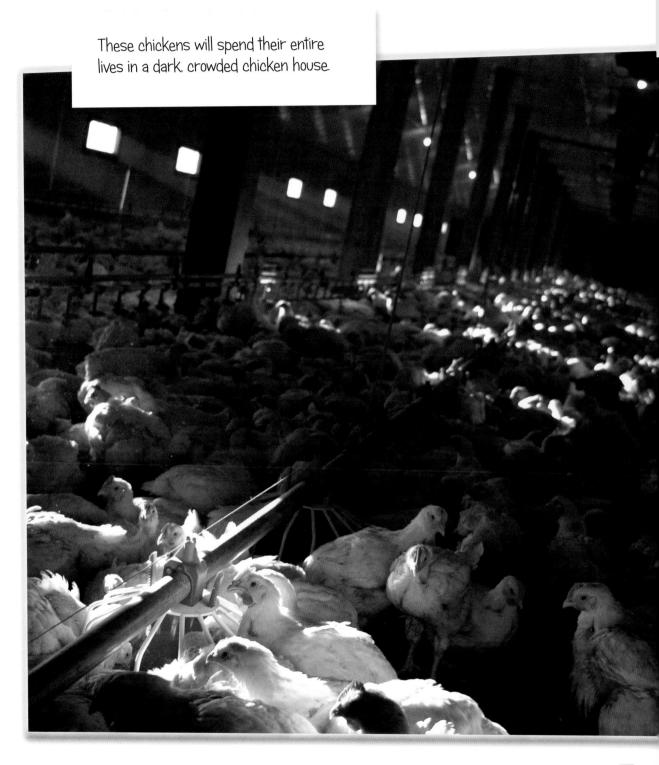

These chickens will spend their entire lives in a dark, crowded chicken house.

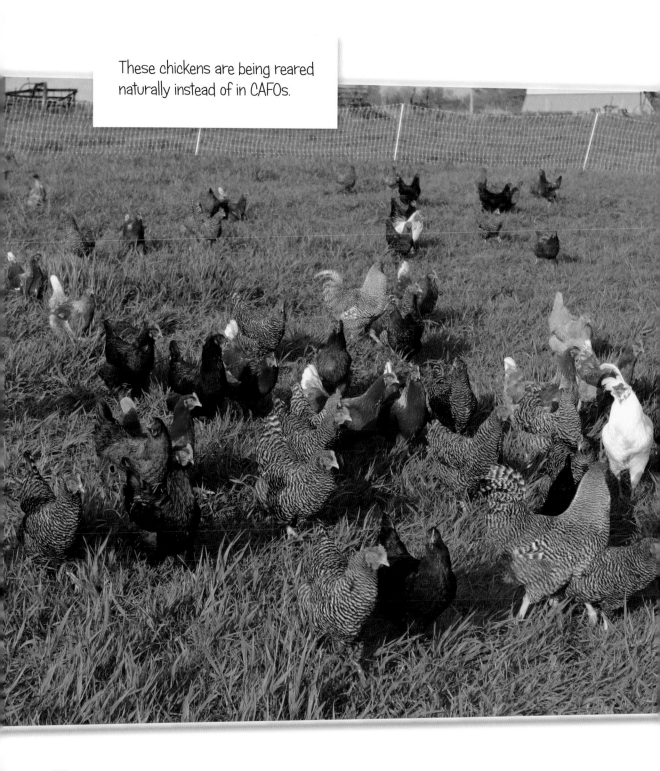

These chickens are being reared naturally instead of in CAFOs.

Free-range chickens

In most parts of the world, the term "free range" means that the chickens spend a good portion of their lives in large outdoor pastures roaming free and eating grass. However, in the United States the term "free range" simply means that the chickens have access to the outdoors. That may mean that there is a small door on one end of a huge chicken house that leads to a dirt or gravel yard. Under these circumstances few of the chickens actually spend any time outdoors, and yet they can still be labelled free range.

Back-garden coops

People who want to keep a few chickens need to have a small coop. There are many different designs for garden coops. Some even look like miniature barns or houses.

Some farmers choose to keep smaller flocks than those in CAFOs. They also may choose not to use antibiotics and other chemicals, preferring to rear their chickens more naturally. Rearing truly free-range chickens is more expensive than keeping chickens in giant chicken houses. Often consumers do not want to pay the difference.

Back-garden chickens

Many families in suburban and even urban neighbourhoods keep small flocks of chickens. Some people allow their chickens to have access to their entire garden, while others build a smaller fenced-in area, not only to keep their chickens in one place, but also to keep them safe from predators.

Chickens in developing countries

Owning a small flock of chickens can make a huge difference for poor families in **developing countries** in Africa, South America, and Asia. Not only do the chickens supply these families with eggs and meat, but they can also be bred, and the chicks can be sold. In some countries in Africa, some women have very little education and few opportunities to make money. Breeding and rearing chickens allows these women to provide for their families.

Migratory duck farming in India

In Kerala, India, duck farmers have found a way to feed their flocks while helping local farmers. After the rice harvest, large flocks of ducks are released into **rice paddies** to eat what is left. Their droppings **fertilize** the soil for the next rice crop.

Chance Christine: Ugandan Chicken Farmer

Keeping chickens has changed Chance Christine's life. Before she began rearing her flock, she was selling porridge by the roadside and was not making enough to feed and clothe her three children. Now her children are clothed, well fed, and going to school.

Each year farmers split their flocks into groups of 500 birds and hire farm labourers to take the ducks on a four-month journey across hundreds of rice fields to the neighbouring state of Tamil Nadu. The ducks eat rice, slugs, and insects in the fields along the way. The rice farmers are given eggs for letting the ducks search for food in their paddies. In Tamil Nadu, mature ducks are sold for their meat, and the rest are trucked back home.

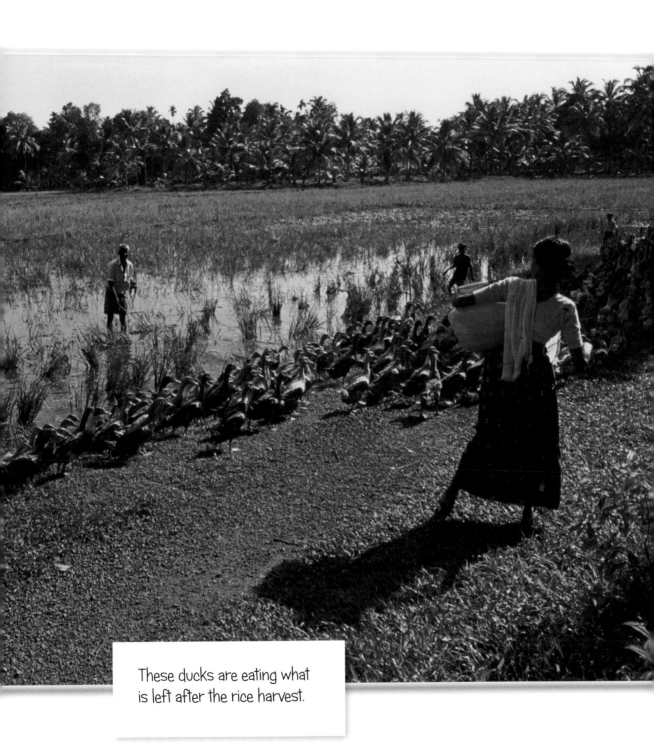

These ducks are eating what
is left after the rice harvest.

How are pigs and sheep farmed?

Pork is one of the most widely eaten meats in the world. Pig products include sausages, ham, and bacon, as well as pork meat. In many developed countries, pigs are reared in huge **CAFOs**. A single CAFO may contain more than 10,000 animals at a time.

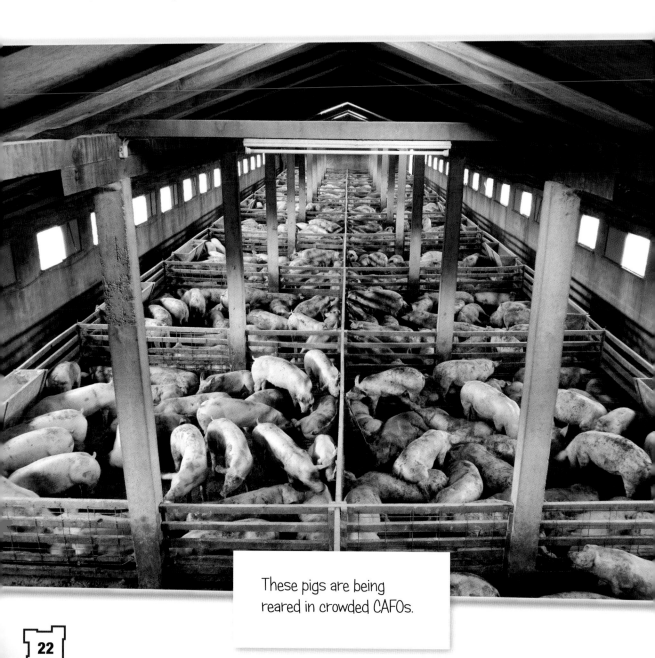

These pigs are being reared in crowded CAFOs.

One of the biggest concerns with large pig farms is the huge amounts of manure that the pigs produce. One hog secretes about 2.7 kilograms (6 pounds) of manure each day. The manure is drained into enormous cesspools, called lagoons. The smell from these lagoons is overpowering and travels for miles. Furthermore, the manure releases toxic fumes that have caused serious health problems in children and the elderly.

China's swine

China produces the most pork by far compared to any other country. Nearly half of all the world's pigs are located in China. Almost all of the pigs in China are reared for domestic consumption. Pig farming in China is **subsidized** by the government. This means that the government gives pig farmers money that they can then spend on housing, feed, and other expenses. Issues of food safety are not unusual in China's pork industry. Farms have been shut down for **unsanitary** conditions and use of illegal drugs.

Smithfield Foods

Smithfield Foods is the world's largest producer of pork. The company is based in Smithfield, Virginia, USA, but has farms and processing plants all over the United States, as well as in several countries, including China, Brazil, Mexico, and the UK.

Pigs in Denmark

Denmark is one of the most successful pig-rearing countries and is the world's largest exporter of pork products. It exports 85 per cent of its pork to 130 different countries.

Denmark has enacted a set of animal welfare laws that have improved the lives of their pigs. These include treatment of mother sows and piglets, living conditions, and transport of the animals. These laws have helped to keep their pigs healthy and the meat they produce safe. In addition, scientists in Denmark are working to reduce the odour from swine waste.

Adopt a pig in Nova Scotia

Maple Lane Farms is a family-owned farm in Nova Scotia, Canada. In the mid-2000s, Maple Lane Farms was losing money due to rising feed costs and low pork prices. It was costing more to rear their pigs than they could get from the meat packers who bought them. The family was nearing **bankruptcy** when they decided to try an "Adopt-a-Pig" scheme.

They soon found that customers were eager to join the scheme. To adopt a pig, the customer paid up front while the pig was still young, and the customer paid more for a pig than the farmers got from the meat packers. However, for that extra money the customer would get meat from a pig that was reared naturally on a farm instead of on a CAFO. After slaughter, the pig was cut and wrapped to the customer's specification and delivered at no extra cost. There are similar schemes on other farms.

Piglets reared on farms outdoors are healthier than those kept in giant CAFOs.

In Australia, sheep are reared on large ranches called stations.

Sheep Down Under

Australia and New Zealand are the world's top sheep producers. Sheep are reared on large ranches called **stations**. Often sheep and cows are reared together on one station. Sheep graze freely on the land until they are ready for slaughter. In Australia a station may be so large that it takes days to round up all the sheep. Well-trained sheep dogs help to herd the sheep. On very large stations, low-flying helicopters may also be used. In New Zealand there are 11 times more sheep than people!

Most people prefer lamb, which means the animal must be slaughtered before it is a year old. Older sheep meat is called mutton. Mutton tends to be tougher and have a stronger flavour.

Sheep dogs

Sheep dogs have been used on large sheep stations in Australia for hundreds of years, and they are still an important part of station life today. They are intelligent, tough, and able to work in hot weather. Sheep dogs herd sheep, round up strays, and keep predators away from the herd.

Bringing back mutton

Mutton was once a popular choice; however, today most people prefer lamb. Meat producers like this trend because it means that they can save money on feed and housing by slaughtering their animals earlier. However, some farmers are bucking this trend. Rather than slaughtering lambs, some farms sell older sheep. They feel that this practice is more **humane** as it allows the sheep to live into adulthood.

What other kinds of meat are farmed?

People in different parts of the world eat all kinds of animal meat. Some of the animals are hunted and some are reared on farms. Animals reared on farms include ostriches, alligators, emus, guinea pigs, turtles, and frogs. In most cases these kinds of animals are kept on small farms, not large **CAFOs**. Often farming animals that are found in the wild keeps people from hunting them. Meats that are not commonly eaten are sometimes called exotic meats.

Eating alligators

Alligators are a part of traditional southern Cajun cuisine (food) in the United States. However, it is illegal to hunt alligators in the United States, so people who enjoy alligator meat must purchase it from farms. Alligator farms in the southern United States often also operate as tourist attractions. Visitors can see some of the alligators in special viewing areas.

Breeding and rearing alligators is not easy. Alligator farmers must follow strict regulations and keep careful records of every alligator they breed. An alligator egg takes about 60 days to hatch. After hatching, the babies live in rearing tanks for a few months. When they are about 0.6 metre (2 feet) long, they are moved to growing houses. In order to grow large fast, alligators must be kept in a hot environment — around 32°C (90°F) — and frequently fed on meat-based meal. Once an alligator is 1.5 to 2 metres (5 to 7 feet) long, it is ready to be slaughtered for its meat, hide, and teeth.

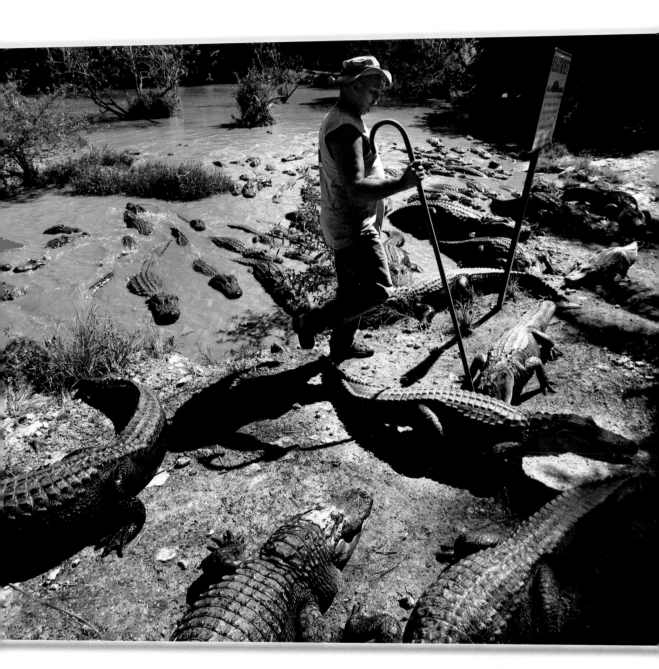

These alligators are being farmed for their meat, hides (skins), and teeth.

Guinea pigs for dinner

Guinea pigs are part of the cuisine in Peru and other Latin American countries. In Peru about 65 million guinea pigs are eaten every year. Guinea pig meat can be found in restaurants, fresh or frozen in the shops, or even live in the markets.

Rearing guinea pigs is not difficult or expensive. Rather than eating expensive feed, guinea pigs can live on alfalfa, corn husks, and table scraps. Guinea pigs have been bred to grow big and fat – up to 3.2 kilograms (7 pounds)! Peruvian women who were previously living in **poverty** are now making money rearing guinea pigs. Guinea pig meat is also being exported to Japan, the United States, and several European countries.

These guinea pigs are not pets. They are bred to be eaten.

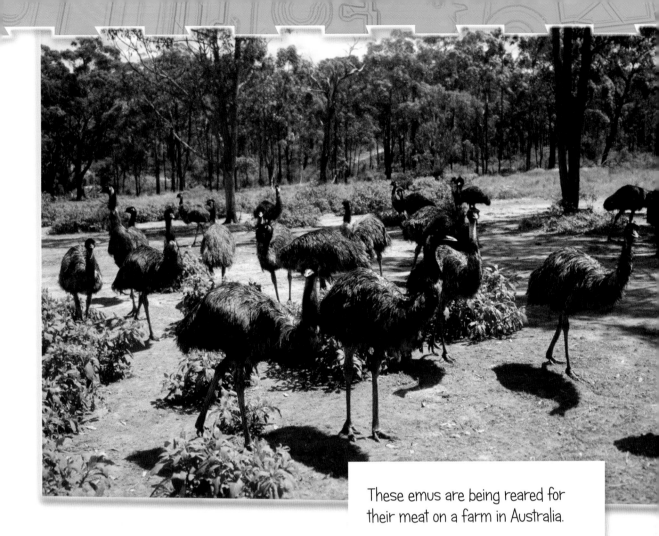

These emus are being reared for their meat on a farm in Australia.

Emu farms in Australia

An emu is a large, flightless bird native to Australia. **Aboriginal people** have been eating emus for thousands of years. Today, emus in the wild are a protected species, so only emus reared on farms may be eaten.

Emus are farmed in every Australian state. There are now about 250 emu farms in Australia. Emus are kept in large, open-air pens and fed grain to supplement the leaves and grass they eat during the day. A fully-grown emu is around 2 metres (over 6 feet tall). It takes about 14 months to raise an emu for slaughter. Emu farms are environmentally friendly because farmers do not need to clear any land to raise emus, and their soft feet do not destroy the land.

What are the negative aspects of the meat industry?

There are more people in the world than ever before, and many of them like to eat meat. It takes a great deal of land, energy, and other resources to rear enough animals to meet the world's demand. **CAFOs** are able to rear large numbers of animals cheaply. However, many agree that rearing animals on large factory farms is cruel to the animals, unhealthy for the humans who consume them, and harmful to the planet.

Animal ethics

Animals raised on large CAFOs are crowded together in large, windowless, warehouse-like buildings. The animals have little room to move and are often forced to live in their own waste. Crowded, **unsanitary** conditions make for many sick animals. Ten per cent of animals in CAFOs die from stress or disease before they are old enough for slaughter. Many people feel it is **unethical** to treat animals this way and refuse to eat meat that comes from CAFOs.

Temple Grandin

Temple Grandin was born in 1947 with **autism**. She believes that this gives her insight into how animals think and feel. Unlike most people, Grandin thinks in pictures instead of words. Grandin has dedicated her life to creating more **humane** ways to keep, transport, and slaughter animals. Today, nearly half the cattle in Canada and the United States are processed in facilities that were designed by Grandin. Grandin has written several important books about autism and animal behaviour. In 2010 an award-winning film was made about her life, starring Claire Danes.

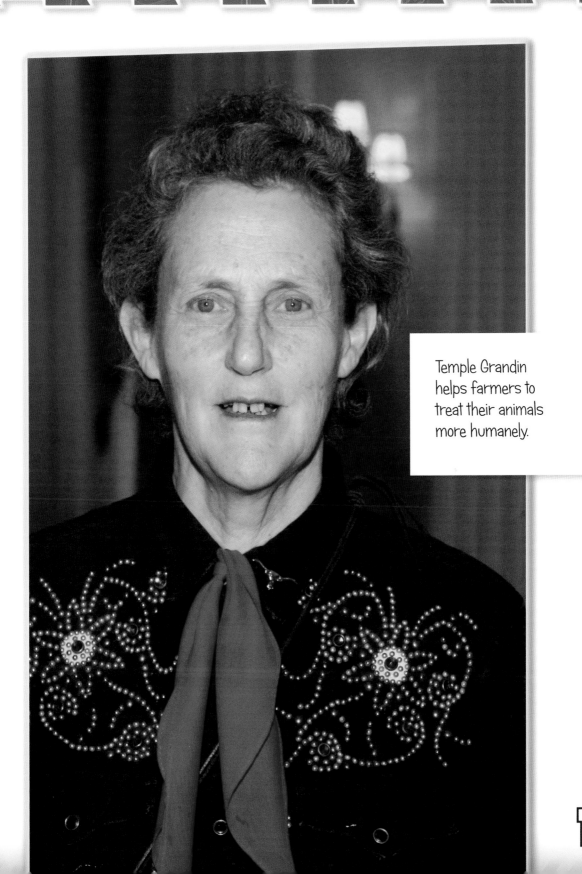

Temple Grandin helps farmers to treat their animals more humanely.

Unhealthy for people

Many people have become ill and even died from eating tainted meat or working with sick animals. Some of the more serious illnesses include: salmonella, E. coli, Creutzfeldt-Jakob disease (CJD), swine flu, and avian flu. In addition, the **antibiotics** and **growth hormones** that are given to animals in CAFOs can cause other serious health problems, such as cancer. This is why these practices have been banned in Europe. Furthermore, working on a ranch or in a slaughterhouse is extremely dangerous. Many workers have been injured or killed.

These chickens have all died because of unsanitary conditions and cannot be eaten.

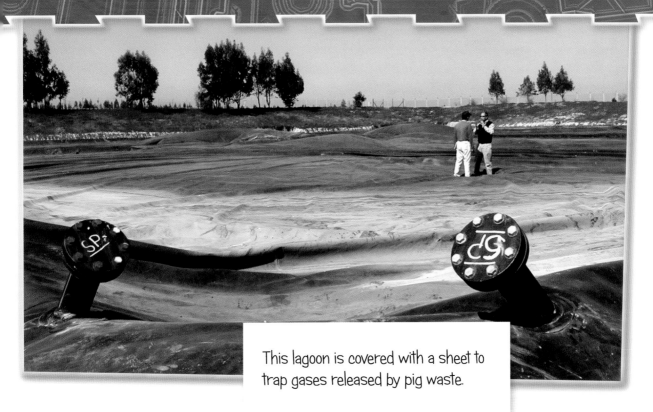

This lagoon is covered with a sheet to trap gases released by pig waste.

Environmental issues

Large amounts of land are needed to graze cattle and to grow grain to feed cattle and other animals that are reared for meat. Nearly one-third of the world's landmass is used for rearing **livestock**. Often, rainforests are cleared to create this land. Rainforests help to prevent **global warming** by absorbing carbon dioxide in the air.

Meat production contributes to global warming in other ways, too. Worldwide, the meat industry accounts for 18 per cent of the planet's **greenhouse gas** emissions. That is more than all the world's cars, boats, planes, and trains combined, which only contribute 13 per cent. Part of these emissions is in the form of **nitrous oxide**, which comes from the manure these animals produce. Another part comes from the **methane gas** that cattle release in large amounts every day. More emissions are created by the transportation of feed for the animals to eat, transportation to the slaughterhouses, and transportation of the meat products themselves to shops and restaurants.

What is the future for livestock farming?

Many factors will affect how the **livestock** industry grows. As the world's population increases, demand for meat will also increase. However, resources such as energy, land, and water are becoming scarcer. While many more people are eating meat than ever before, **vegetarianism** is also a growing trend. People may stop eating meat to improve their own health or the health of the planet, or because they do not want to contribute to the **unethical** treatment of animals.

Stricter regulations

The future is also likely to bring stricter regulations about how **CAFO** operators treat their animals and manage waste. Routine use of **antibiotics** in livestock has been banned in Europe, as well as the use of **growth hormones** for cattle. Similar bans may be introduced in the United States. Improvements in the meat industry are likely to come at a price. Consumers will have to pay more for the meat that they buy.

Sustainable farming

With more people demanding ethical treatment of animals and better management of the land, **sustainable farms** are on the rise. Small farmers continue to find ways to rear animals with minimal environmental impact. Rearing livestock in a natural way costs considerably more than keeping them on factory farms. However, many people are willing to pay more money for meat that they know was reared ethically without hormones and antibiotics.

The cattle here are eating feed that has been ground and mixed on the farm.

Grain grinder and mixer

While large CAFOs buy pre-mixed grain, some small farms grind and mix their own grains in machines to make the perfect food for their animals.

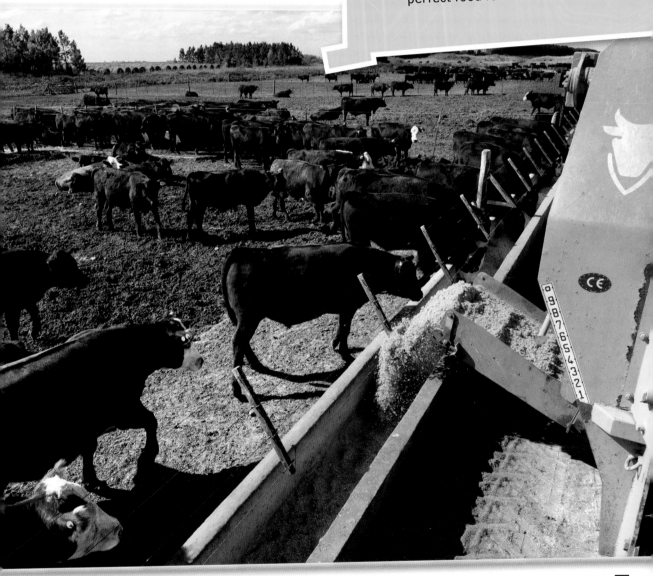

More meat for developing countries

As **developing countries** get richer, their meat consumption increases. Many families that were once too poor to afford much meat now find that they have enough money to have meat with every meal.

Smaller farms are helping to fill this demand for more meat. Some groups are helping poor people to start rearing livestock by giving them small loans to buy animals and educating them about how to care for them. New technologies, such as improving the quality of foraging grasses, are being created specifically for these small farmers.

Athol Klieve: Research Scientist

Australian scientist Athol Klieve believes that kangaroos may be able to help reduce the amount of **methane gas** released by cattle. Both cattle and kangaroos have **bacteria** in their guts that help to break down the food that they eat. This process produces methane in cows, but in kangaroos it produces acetate – a substance similar to vinegar. Klieve wants to replace the methane-producing bacteria in cattle with the acetate-producing bacteria in kangaroos. This would not only reduce methane gas, but would also give the cattle more energy!

Athol Klieve is working to reduce the amount of methane gas released by cattle.

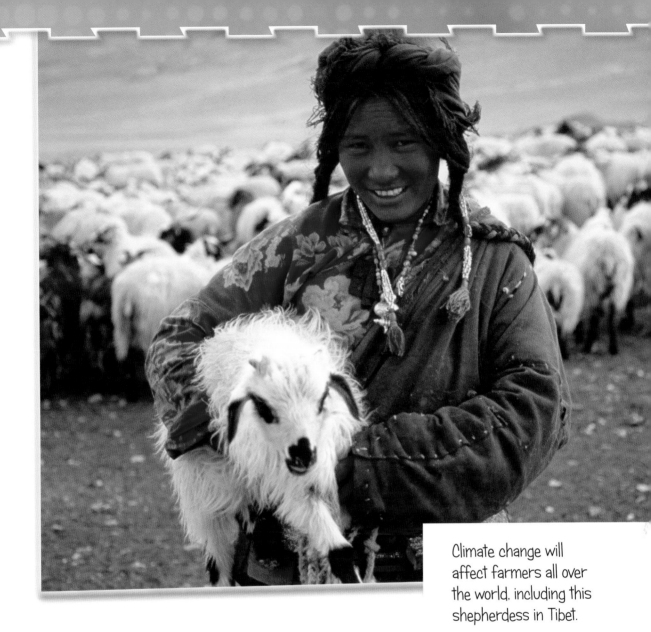

Climate change will affect farmers all over the world, including this shepherdess in Tibet.

Climate change

Global warming will affect livestock farmers all over the world. As the planet gets warmer, there will be changes in the way that livestock feed is grown. It is possible that there will even be feed shortages. There are also likely to be stricter regulations to prevent livestock's contribution to global warming. Restrictions on how much land can be cleared and regulations about emissions from waste and animals are likely to be enacted.

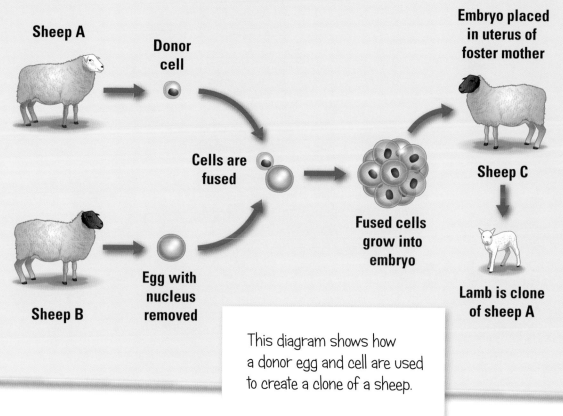

Sheep A

Donor cell

Embryo placed in uterus of foster mother

Cells are fused

Sheep C

Fused cells grow into embryo

Egg with nucleus removed

Sheep B

Lamb is clone of sheep A

This diagram shows how a donor egg and cell are used to create a clone of a sheep.

Science on the farm

Agricultural scientists are working to find more technologies to improve meat production. Although some of these are aimed at raising the quality of life for the animals, most are focused on finding ways to grow bigger animals in a shorter amount of time.

Genetics

Genetics and breeding have already played a huge part in the industry and will continue to do so in the future. Because of **selective breeding**, the animals we eat today are much bigger than those that were eaten a hundred years ago. In the future, scientists may manipulate animal **DNA** with **genetic engineering** to produce animals that grow faster and bigger.

Cloning

Cloning is the process of making a duplicate or identical twin of an animal using the animal's DNA. This is achieved by fusing DNA from an adult animal with an egg that has had the **nucleus** removed, and then implanting the egg into an adult animal's uterus to grow. In the future, cloning could be used to duplicate the best animals on a farm many times in order to improve the stock.

In vitro meat

In vitro meat is animal flesh that has never been a part of a whole, living animal. In vitro meat is grown in labs by taking muscle cells from animals and adding protein to make them grow. Scientists working on in vitro meat hope that the process will become a safer, less expensive, and more **humane** way to produce large amounts of meat.

Dolly the sheep was the first mammal ever to be cloned.

How important is the meat industry?

Meat is a large and important industry. All over the world, billions of animals are being reared for their meat. Over a billion humans are working to get these animals reared, slaughtered, and on to your plate.

CAFO operators and farmers spend their lives managing these animals. Other farmers grow grain to feed these animals. Still more people transport the grain to farms and CAFOs and, when they are ready, transport the animals to the slaughterhouses.

At the slaughterhouses, workers process the animals and pack the meat. Then even more people are needed to transport the meat to shops and restaurants. In addition, there are people who make the tools and equipment needed to rear and process animals, scientists and researchers who work to improve the industry, and inspectors whose job is to make sure that everyone is following meat-industry regulations.

Because the demand for meat is so high, the meat industry faces many challenges. For most of the meat we eat, the welfare of the animals is not always the highest priority to the farmers. In addition, the meat industry is taking a heavy toll on the planet in terms of pollution, global warming, and loss of rainforest.

Eating meat raised on **sustainable farms** is one way to help our planet. Even though sustainable meat is more expensive than factory-farmed meat, many people feel that contented animals and a healthy planet are worth the price.

The cattle here are being reared on a sustainable farm for a healthier planet.

Glossary

Aboriginal people people native to Australia

antibiotic drug that cures or prevents illnesses and infections caused by bacteria

autism mental disorder marked by difficulty in communication and social interactions

bacteria tiny, one-celled organisms; germs

bankruptcy not having enough money

botanist person who studies plants

broiler chicken bred for meat

bubonic plague epidemic disease that killed half the population of Europe in the Middle Ages

cloning process of creating an animal or plant that is an exact copy of another animal or plant

composting using decaying vegetation and manure for fertilizer

concentrated animal feeding operation (CAFO) factory farm used for rearing large numbers of animals in relatively small spaces, usually indoors

developing country poor country that is in the process of becoming more advanced economically

DNA genetic information found in the nucleus of a cell

domesticate to train an animal to live with or work for humans

drought long period without enough rainfall

feedlot area or building where animals are fattened for slaughter

fertilizer substance added to soil to promote plant growth

feudal system system of land ownership and labour in Europe in the Middle Ages

genetic engineering scientific process of changing a plant or animal by combining pieces of genetic material (DNA) from different species.

global warming gradual increase of the planet's temperature caused by increasing amounts of pollution

greenhouse gas gas that contributes to global warming by absorbing radiation

growth hormone substance that regulates the growth of plants or animals

humane compassion or sympathy for animal or human welfare

incubator equipment used for keeping eggs warm until they hatch

indigenous native to a place

livestock animals kept on a farm

methane gas colourless, odourless gas that contributes to global warming

nitrous oxide colourless gas that contributes to global warming

nomadic moving frequently from place to place

nucleus central part of a cell that contains genetic information

organic reared naturally without the use of synthetic chemicals

pesticide chemical used for killing insects or other pests, especially on plants

poultry domestic birds reared for their meat or eggs

poverty when a person does not have enough money for food, shelter, and basic needs

rice paddy flooded field where rice is grown

station large ranch in Australia or New Zealand

selective breeding intentionally producing animals or plants with desired traits

subsidized to give financial support

sustainable farm farm that uses methods that do not harm the environment

temperament general way in which a person or animal reacts and behaves

trait specific quality

unethical morally wrong

unsanitary dirty, unhealthy, and likely to cause disease

vegetarianism diet that does not include any meat

Find out more

Books

Farming for the Future (Planet SOS), Gerry Bailey (Gareth Stevens Publishing, 2011)

Farming in the Future (Food and Farming), Ian Graham (Wayland, 2011)

Food, Laura Buller (DK Publishing, 2005)

Local Farms and Sustainable Foods (Save the Planet), Julia Vogel (Cherry Lake, 2010)

Maasai (Indigenous Peoples), Rennay Craats (Weigl, 2005)

Sustainable Farming (How Can We Save Our World?), Carol Ballard (Franklin Watts, 2009)

The Food Industry (Global Industries Uncovered), Rob Bowden (Wayland, 2009)

Websites

The Soil Association

Find out everything you need to know about the meaning of "organic", the overuse of antibiotics in farm animals, and new trends in sustainable farming on this excellent website.

www.soilassociation.org

Factory Farms

Learn about the dark side of factory farms and about sustainable farming from this site that includes a video talk from an informed eleven year old.

tiki.oneworld.net/food/food3.html

All about animals

Visit this website to find out everything you ever wanted to know about animals including farm animals and factory farming. You also get a chance to vote on the sort of farming you would prefer to see happen.

www.allaboutanimals.org.uk/SP-FactoryFarming.asp

Compassion in World Farming

This website explains the aims of CIW, and provides news of its campaigns against cruelty to farm animals.

www.ciwf.org.uk/farm_animals

Places to visit

Museums

There are many local museums of rural life that give you a good idea of farming practices in the past. You can find your nearest museum by searching on the internet.

www.britainsfinest.co.uk/museums/search_results.cfm/searchclasscode/435

Farmers' markets

Use the website below to find a farmers' market near you. At many farmers' markets, you can talk to farmers who might be able to tell you more about their farming practices.

www.local-farmers-markets.co.uk

Agricultural shows

A great way to see farm animals and all the latest farm machinery is to visit an agricultural show. These shows often have livestock competitions and other agricultural events as well. Check on the internet to find a show near you that welcomes visitors.

Index